21 Keys to Better Work/Life Balance
Unlock Your Full Potential
Workbook

Copyright © 2013 by Michael Thomas Sunnarborg

All rights reserved. No part of this publication may be reproduced in whole or in part – other than "fair use" as either brief quotations or in a review – without expressed written permission from the author. Select names in this publication have been used with permission. All other names are fictitious and any resemblance to real persons, living or dead, is purely coincidental.

The intent of this book is to offer information of a general nature to help support physical, emotional, and spiritual well-being. The author assumes no responsibility for any actions as a result of reading and/or applying any of the information or recommendations presented in this book.

Original cover design and illustrations by Lukas J. Dickie

Workbook design and layout by Becky Wontor

Printed by CreateSpace

Distributed by Creative Consulting

Find copies of this book online at
21keystoworklifebalance.com

ISBN 978-0-9854503-5-9
10 9 8 7 6 5 4 3 2 1

21 Keys
to
Work/Life
Balance

Workbook

*Unlock Your
Full Potential*

Michael Thomas Sunnarborg

Introduction	**1**
Chapter 1: Welcome to Awareness	**3**
Key 1: The Balance Myth	4
Key 2: Choice	5
Key 3: Intention	6
Key 4: Frequency	7
Key 5: Strengths	8
Key 6: Power	9
Key 7: Know Thyself	10
Chapter 2: Moving Into Alignment	**11**
Key 8: Communication	12
Key 9: Boundaries	13
Key 10: Environment	14
Key 11: Purpose	15
Key 12: Relationships	16
Key 13: Trust	17
Key 14: Appreciation	18
Chapter 3: The Key is Activation	**19**
Key 15: Begin Within	20
Key 16: Human Being, Human Doing	21
Key 17: Live Your Passion on Purpose	22
Key 18: Manage the Leader Within	23
Key 19: Soften Your Stance	24
Key 20: Work Smarter, Not Harder	25
Key 21: Go With the Flow	26
Closing	**27**

Introduction

Welcome to the companion workbook for *21 Keys to Work/Life Balance: Unlock Your Full Potential.* This workbook contains each of the Balance Plan questions and Key Actuators from the book themes, and has been designed to assist you with creating your Balance Plan. If you haven't yet had a chance to read *21 Keys to Work/Life Balance,* you can find links to the books at: 21keystoworklifebalance.com

📖 Balance Plan questions

🔑 Key Actuator

Start by thinking of an area in your life where you'd like to create better balance and then use the workbook to document your answers to the daily questions. Your plan can help shed light on the situation and support you in brainstorming potential solutions.

You might find it useful to journal about the questions, or simply mull them over during your day. They can also serve as a useful meditation focus; simply bring the questions into your mind during your regular meditation practice and notice the thoughts that float up in response. The Key Actuator is a "to-do" activity designed to help you apply the lessons from each theme. Putting theory into action helps integrate the concepts directly into your experience.

Remember: The power to make changes in your life is *always* in your hands. Make a commitment to paying closer attention to your priorities at work and at home and create the momentum for better work/life balance in your life today. It's your choice.

To your best balanced life!
Michael Thomas Sunnarborg

Chapter 1: Welcome to Awareness

*To become different from what we are,
we must have some awareness of what we are.*
Eric Hoffer

We are always learning. Our powerful consciousness is absorbing and processing everything in our environment—including information, sights, sounds, and smells—whether we realize it or not. From our experiences we make choices using the power of our thoughts, feelings, and intuition. In order to find better work/life balance, we must first become aware of the factors that influence our lives on a daily basis.

The first seven keys focus on awareness. Raising our awareness reminds us that the power to influence our work/life balance always begins with noticing what's happening in the present moment.

Key 1: The Balance Myth
Awareness

> *There is no secret to balance.*
> *You just have to feel the waves.*
> Frank Herbert

📖 How does your current focus at work and home balance out? What's working well? What's not?

📖 What are some things you are doing to create a better blend between your work and life?

🔑 **One + One**

This week, write down one thing you'd like to *stop* doing and one thing you'd like to *start* doing to help bring better balance between your work and home life. For example, *I will stop checking my email every ten minutes*, and, *I will start taking a 30-minute walk each day*. Put this list where you can see it—on your laptop, iPad, desktop, or sticky note in your car—and make a commitment to changing *only* those two things this week.

Key 2: Choice
Awareness

> *I believe that we are solely responsible for our choices,
> and we have to accept the consequences of every deed,
> word, and thought throughout our lifetime.*
> Elisabeth Kubler-Ross

📖 How have your choices affected your overall health and well-being at home? At work?

📖 In what ways can you use your power to start choosing something different?

🗝 **Choose Consciously**

Take a moment this week to prioritize two important things: tasks and people. Take a short inventory of your tasks and ask yourself: Which tasks do I need to spend more time on? Where should I reduce my time? Now take inventory of your relationships: Whom do I need to spend more time with? From whom do I need to detach or take a step back? Add these decisions to your calendar or to-do list for the coming week.

Key 3: Intention

> *Don't confuse having a career with having a life.*
> Hillary Rodham Clinton

📖 How do your intentions support you in your current job? In your personal life?

📖 In what ways could clarifying your intentions help create desirable outcomes?

🗝 **Mention Your Intention**

Intentions take life when we speak them out loud or write them down. Take a moment this week to think of your intentions for your career and your personal life, write them down, and then share them with someone you trust. Throughout the week, notice how your attitudes, actions, and words are either helping to fulfill your intentions or moving you away from them. If needed, make necessary changes to put yourself back on track.

Key 4: Frequency
Awareness

> *You do not attract what you want.*
> *You attract what you are.*
> Dr. Wayne Dyer

📖 What do you know about your personal frequency? When do you need counter-balancing from others?

📖 What do you notice about the frequencies of the people in your workplace? How can adjusting your frequency help you to blend better with others?

🗝 **Do You Hear That?**

This week, pay attention to the frequencies around you. What does it feel like when someone's frequency is similar to yours? What happens when someone's frequency is not like yours? How do you adjust to people's different frequencies? Write an example in your journal this week about how the frequency of someone else played an important role in contributing your sense of balance or lack of balance.

Key 5: Strengths Awareness

> *Balance, peace, and joy are the fruit of a successful life. It starts with recognizing your talents and finding ways to serve others by using them.*
> Thomas Kinkade

📖 How has being aware of your strengths helped you in your job? In your personal life?

📖 What strengths do you have that you're not using? Why not? What do you think would happen if you focused on them?

🗝 **Creative Challenge**

This week, think of something that you enjoy doing and that you do well. How often do you have the chance to do it? How can you add more of it to your work and life? For example, if you like graphic design and it's not part of your job, perhaps you can add some graphics to your status reports, presentations, or meeting agendas? Or maybe there's a chance for you to use your talents in a special event or project? Be willing to see how creative you can be about integrating your strengths and talents into what you already do.

Key 6: Power
Awareness

> *What it lies in our power to do,*
> *it lies in our power not to do.*
> Aristotle

📖 How does power show up in your relationships at work? At home? How are they similar or different?

📖 When do you experience the most personal power? How does that affect the rest of your life?

🗝 **Power Play**

Think of a time when you felt powerful. What happened? What were you doing? Who were you with? If the memory was a personal experience, imagine translating that same feeling of power to a work experience or vice-versa. Now what does it feel like? What are you doing? Who are you with? What would it take for you to feel more powerful in this area of your life? What would you do or say differently? How can you apply this experience to change the balance of power in your life this week?

Key 7: Know Thyself
Awareness

> *I am larger, better than I thought.*
> *I did not know I held so much goodness.*
> Walt Whitman

📖 In what ways could you know yourself better? What parts of you seem undeveloped, hidden, or mysterious?

📖 In what ways are you taking care of yourself? How are you neglecting yourself?

🔑 **Me Time**

This week, schedule some time on your calendar for yourself—"me time." During this time, focus your energy on *yourself*. Allow yourself to drift into whatever you want—just don't do what you'd consider "work." Instead, read a book, go for a walk, listen to music, watch a movie—do something for yourself. As my good friend and fellow coach Honoree Corder says, "If it's not on the calendar, it's not happening!" Notice how time for yourself affects your sense of balance and equilibrium.

Chapter 2: Moving Into Alignment

Awareness

> *Tug on anything at all and you'll find it
> connected to everything else in the universe.*
> John Muir

Moving into alignment is the second stage to finding better work/life balance. Alignment happens both inside and outside of us. As we move in and out of alignment with our deepest self, our surroundings directly reflect our present state of balance. If we stay connected to our thoughts, feelings, and intuition, we understand more clearly what our true alignment is and find that alignment more easily.

The next seven keys will help you take a closer look at alignment. Focusing on alignment reminds us that a major influence on our work/life balance is the ability to consciously bring ourselves into alignment with the people and places that connect us with our deepest sense of purpose.

Key 8: Communication
Alignment

> *I've never regretted the things I said nearly as much as the words I left unspoken.*
> Lisa Kleypas

📖 How is your communication different at work than in your personal life? How is it similar?

📖 How can your personal communication style be clearer and more effective?

🗝 **Talk To Me**

Strengthen your communication this week by becoming a good speaker or a good listener. Find a friend, co-worker, or family member and tell them that you are practicing communication skills. If you are naturally a talker, then you will only listen. If you are already a good listener, then you will only speak. Set a timer for 15 minutes and have either you or the other person speak uninterrupted for the entire 15 minutes. The subject can be anything at all. If you are the listener, do not speak—listen attentively. If you are the speaker, let your ideas and thoughts flow. What did you notice? How did this exercise affect the rest of your communication this week?

Key 9: Boundaries

Respect yourself and others will respect you.
Confucius

📖 How have you established your personal boundaries at work? In your personal life?

📖 Where do your boundaries need strengthening? Where could your boundaries be more flexible?

🔑 **That's My Limit**

Take a moment to think about a recent situation at home or work where you felt your boundaries were crossed. What happened? How did you react and what was the result? Now think of a time when you pushed someone to their limit and they let you know. How did you know that you crossed their boundary? What happened after that, and how did it change your relationship? Add these insights to your journal.

Key 10: Environment

> *Our environment, the world in
> which we live and work, is a mirror of
> our attitudes and expectations.*
> Earl Nightingale

📖 Which things in your present work environment are supporting you? Which aren't? What about in your home environment?

📖 How could you shift your environments, even just a little, so that they better support your intentions?

🔑 **Here Today, Gone to Maui**

Take a moment to remember your last trip away from home. It could've been a long vacation to a far away destination, or just a weekend away. Where did you go? What did you do? Why did you take this trip? Now reflect on how the contrast of that environment shifted your perspective. Did you feel relief? Or perhaps you felt uncomfortable being away from home? And when you returned from your trip, how did you feel? Relaxed? Refreshed? When you change your environment, your environment changes you. This week, think about how a shift in your environment—whether small or large—will affect you.

Key 11: Purpose

> *People take different roads seeking fulfillment and happiness. Just because they're not on your road doesn't mean they've gotten lost.*
> Dalai Lama

How often do you feel a sense of purpose? How does your current job support, clarify, and strengthen your purpose?

What can you do to strengthen your sense of purpose in your career? In your personal life?

Purpose Points

Stop and think about the last time you felt a strong sense of purpose. Perhaps it was when you were assigned a very important task, or maybe it was to be of support to someone when they needed it. This week, recognize and make note of those experiences where you feel a sense of purpose and be grateful for those moments. Write them down in a gratitude journal or make a thankful list.

Key 12: Relationships
Alignment

> *Our greatest joy and our greatest pain come in our relationships with others.*
> Stephen R. Covey

📖 How are your relationships at home and work serving you? How are they similar? How are they different?

📖 What changes could you make in your relationships to bring them into closer alignment with your intentions and purpose?

🗝 **Pass It On**

Think of a relationship that's had a powerful impact on you and your life. This person may be a teacher, coach, friend, or parent—someone whose words or actions have made a lasting impression on you. Next, write down what you received from them. For example, in my life I was uplifted and encouraged by my high school music teacher, Mrs. Bradley. Mrs. Bradley believed in me and my talents, taught me to express my creative and musical self with confidence, and allowed me the opportunity to let my light shine for others to see. Repeat this exercise thinking of other people who've had significant impact on your life.

Key 13: Trust
Alignment

> *Sometimes you cannot believe what you see;*
> *you have to believe what you feel.*
> Mitch Albom

📖 How does trust play a significant role in your current job? In your personal life? How do these levels of trust differ? How are they similar?

📖 Where do you trust yourself, and where do you feel out of alignment with yourself?

🗝 **In We I Trust**

Take a moment this week to evaluate your relationships. Choose one area where you would like to a) develop more trust in someone; and b) behave in a more trustworthy way. Now list the ways in which the person in scenario a) IS trustworthy. What can you trust them for? Make a list of these things and add to it throughout the week. For scenario b), what can you be trusted for? Make a list and add to it throughout the week. Placing your attention on trust will help to develop it.

Key 14: Appreciation

> *Among the things you can give and still keep are your word, a smile, and a grateful heart.*
> Zig Ziglar

📖 How does it feel when someone genuinely appreciates you at work? At home? What effect does it have on your confidence or self-esteem?

📖 What happens when you show your appreciation for other people? How do you feel?

🗝 **Treasure Hunt**

Think about someone in your life who challenges you—a friend, family member, co-worker, boss—someone who is driving you crazy, or someone with whom you just don't get along. Now put that person in your mind's eye, and begin to think of something—anything—that you genuinely appreciate about them. Even if it takes a while, come up with a list of at least three things. There's buried treasure in there somewhere! Focus on those things the next time you speak with that person. With time and patience, notice how this simple act of unspoken appreciation changes your relationship.

Chapter 3: The Key is Activation

> *Nothing happens until something moves.*
> Albert Einstein

Awareness brings attention to the critical factors influencing our work/life balance; alignment helps us focus our energy; activation puts theory into practice and ideas into motion. Without activation, good ideas are only ideas. Activation is the key to implementation and the third stage to finding better work/life balance.

The next seven keys are opportunities for activation. Focusing on activation helps us make changes in our lives and reminds us that finding a healthy blend between our work and personal activities depends on our ability to take action.

Key 15: Begin Within
Activation

> *Do not go where the path may lead, go instead where there is no path and leave a trail.*
> Ralph Waldo Emerson

📖 When have you had an intuitive nudge about something or someone? How did you act on it? How did it turn out?

📖 Where is your intuition leading you right now? What inner knowledge are you tempted to ignore?

🔑 **Listen Up**

This week, pay attention to your intuition. Whether you are engaged in a conversation at home or at work, focus on what your intuition is saying to you. If you are at work and sitting in a meeting, notice how there is an internal dialogue going on inside of you as well as the one outside of you. What are you thinking and feeling about the topic of discussion? What is your intuition telling you? Take a moment to jot down what comes to mind.

Key 16: Human Being, Human Doing

Activation

> *You find peace not by rearranging the circumstances of your life, but by realizing who you are at the deepest level.*
> Eckhart Tolle

📖 In what ways is your "doing" defining who you are at work? In your personal life?

📖 How are you "being" at work? At home? How do you want to be?

🔑 **Who You Be?**

Take time this week to make a list of the most important or influential people in your life right now—both personal and professional—and then answer the following questions: How do the people who know you personally see you differently than those who know you professionally? What is different? What feels true? What feels false or inauthentic? How is your "doing" tied to your personality in these relationships? How is your "being"? Notice if you feel consistency or inconsistency in the way others perceive you. What is this saying about you?

Key 17: Live Your Passion on Purpose

Activation

> *Always remember, you have within you the strength, the patience, and the passion to reach for the stars and to change the world.*
> Harriet Tubman

📖 Where is the passion in your work? In your personal life?

📖 What would you do if you didn't have to earn a living? How can you bring that passion more fully into your life now?

🗝 **Passion Pursuit**

Take a moment to find your passion by asking yourself the following questions: "What do I really love to do? What have I done in the past that I was really good at?" Spend the week noticing or remembering what you love and why it matters, and then take the inquiry one step deeper and ask what these things have in common. What do they share? Often, that is where deeper passion lies.

Key 18: Manage the Leader Within

Activation

> *If you seek to lead, invest at least 50% of your
> time leading yourself—your own purpose,
> ethics, principles, motivation, conduct.*
> Dee Hock

📖 In what ways have you been leading yourself effectively? What are your strengths as a leader of others?

📖 How is your self-leadership connected to the way you lead others? How are they different?

🗝 **Practice What You Teach**

This week, notice every time you give someone else advice or make a suggestion. Keep a list for a day or two. Then, try following each piece of advice you've given. What happens?

Key 19: Soften Your Stance

Activation

> *A man wrapped up in himself makes a very small bundle.*
> Benjamin Franklin

📖 Where could you soften your stance? What might change if you did?

📖 In what ways have you observed changes in the responses of others depending on your approach? Why is this important to recognize?

🔑 **How's That Working For You?**

Think of a current situation in your life where you are not getting the results you desire, and take a moment to answer the following questions: What is your intention (desired result)? How important is it that you get your result? What are you willing to give up or compromise in order to get it? What other perspectives have you considered? How might softening your stance get you the desired result or something even better? Sometimes, the approach we're taking to achieve something works for *us* but is not necessarily the best approach for all concerned.

Key 20: Work Smarter, Not Harder

Activation

> The major work of the world is not done
> by geniuses. It is done by ordinary people,
> with balance in their lives, who have learned
> to work in an extraordinary manner.
> Gordon B. Hinckley

📖 How might you work more efficiently in your job? At home?

📖 In what ways could doing things differently help you work and live smarter in your personal life?

🔑 **Start, Stop, Continue**

Take a moment to list some of your "good" and "bad" habits. What are you doing that's working for you? What is not? What would you like to start doing differently? What are your intentions? Goals? Ideal situations? Now take a sheet of paper and make three columns: Start, Stop, Continue, and place each habit in one of the categories accordingly:

- **Start** = What you are neglecting or not doing (i.e., exercise)
- **Stop** = What is unproductive (i.e., negative self-talk)
- **Continue** = What is healthy (i.e., healthy food choices)

By taking the time to start, stop, and continue habits, you will have a better idea of how to reprioritize your energies to work and live smarter.

Key 21: Go With the Flow
Activation

> *It's not your work to make anything happen.*
> *It's your work to dream it and let it happen.*
> Abraham Hicks

📖 In which areas of your life are you allowing or resisting? Of your work?

📖 How might you let go and go with the flow? What would you be risking? What might change?

🗝 **Flip It**

Many of us compare our emotional state to that of a roller coaster going up and down. We say we're feeling "up" or "down." This week, try flipping it: instead of using vertical orientation—up and down, use horizontal—out and in. Feeling happy might feel expanded like breathing out, while feeling unhappy might feel compressed like holding in your breath. Feeling expanded or compressed carries less judgment than up or down and is not as dramatic as a roller coaster. That, in itself, is a more balanced and gentle approach to understanding emotions. Besides, this perspective allows you to exhale and let go.

Closing

> *The best and safest thing is to keep a balance in your life,*
> *acknowledge the great powers around us and in us.*
> Euripides

Now that you've read each of the keys, answered the questions, and performed the activities, I encourage you to apply what you've learned to help unlock your full potential. At any time, you can create a new Balance Plan to help shift any aspect of either your work or personal life as you choose. Remember: The power to make changes in your life is *always* in your hands.

My challenge to you is to see yourself as a whole person—that your work is an extension of you and an opportunity for you to create yourself in a way that serves the world and the people in it. When you recognize that your gifts and talents were meant to be shared, you will step into the full potential you were always meant to experience. Once you realize that life is truly about the adventure of creating yourself, you will be able to live in the present moment more peacefully and joyfully than ever before—regardless of your circumstances.

I believe in you, and I believe you can make anything happen. Focus on what you truly desire. Be brave. Be bold. Savor the moments and memories with those around you. Live life to its fullest, and believe that your life has meaning and purpose. And remember, along your journey, to keep applying what you learn about yourself and others to experience better balance in your work and life.

About the Author

Michael Thomas Sunnarborg, Ambassador of Goodwill, is a speaker, author, and wellness coach. He has spent much of his life traveling and living in different parts of the world including Europe, Asia, and the South Pacific. His travel blogs and photo galleries have been followed by thousands of readers worldwide.

Michael is the author of *21 Days to Better Balance*, *21 Steps to Better Relationships*, and *21 Keys to Work/Life Balance*—a series of books and workshops designed to help people find better balance and happiness in their lives. He is also the author of photography books, one of which—*Inspiration from the World*—highlights moments of inspiration as he traveled to 16 countries in 12 months. Selected images from the book are licensed by National Geographic.

Michael currently resides in St. Paul, Minnesota. In addition to writing, Michael gives a variety of presentations and workshops to national and international audiences. He spends a large portion of his time traveling to new destinations, meeting new people, eating new foods, and swapping stories.

For information on coaching, presentations, and workshops given by Michael Thomas Sunnarborg, visit michaelsunnarborg.com

Other books by Michael Thomas Sunnarborg:

21 Keys to Work/Life Balance

*21 Steps to Better Relationships:
Find More Balance with Others*

21 Steps to Better Relationships Workbook

*21 Days to Better Balance:
Find More Balance in a Busy World*

21 Days to Better Balance Workbook

Inspiration from the World

Order additional copies of this book and eBook at:

21keystoworklifebalance.com

Namaste